THE ULTIMATE GUIDE TO GOOGLE AI STUDIO

Unlock AI's Full Potential

Dr.Rajnish Kumawat

ISBN:9798308292999

Cover design by: Art Painter

Printed in the United States of America

CONTENTS

INTRODUCTION

Imagine a world where artificial intelligence is not just a futuristic concept but a tool readily available to anyone with an idea. This is the reality we are stepping into—an era of unprecedented possibilities where AI is reshaping how we live, work, and create. From the algorithms that personalize our online experiences to the sophisticated systems that power medical breakthroughs, AI is rapidly becoming an integral part of our daily lives. This technological transformation presents both opportunities and challenges, demanding that we all become more familiar and comfortable with the potential and pitfalls of AI.

At the heart of this revolution is Google AI Studio—a platform that democratizes access to cutting-edge AI models, making them intuitive and user-friendly. It's more than just a collection of algorithms; it is a canvas where you can explore, experiment, and bring your AI ideas to life. Whether you want to generate creative text, create stunning images, or build intelligent conversational chatbots, Google AI Studio provides a versatile environment to turn your vision into reality. It enables both novices and experts to test new technologies and implement creative solutions without the need for extensive programming experience or expensive computational resources.

Google AI Studio is designed to bridge the gap between complex AI models and practical applications. It offers a simplified interface for interacting with AI capabilities and provides the necessary tools to iterate and improve your projects. What makes AI Studio particularly powerful is its ability to handle a range of tasks, including text generation, text analysis, image creation, image processing, and more, all within a single, cohesive platform. It allows you to develop rapidly, test rigorously and adapt to new requirements.

This book is designed to serve as your comprehensive guide to Google AI Studio. We'll start by laying the foundation with basic AI concepts, and then delve into the specifics of using the platform for various tasks. You will discover how to harness the power of text-based models for writing compelling content, how to generate stunning visuals with image AI, how to build conversational chatbots, and much more. We'll also explore how to manage, integrate, and deploy your projects using this tool and other technologies. We'll also explore best practices, common pitfalls, and how to deploy your projects to the real world.

This book has been prepared with the information available up to its publication date. Please be aware that Google AI Studio is a continuously evolving platform. Therefore, some features, functionalities, and menu names may differ slightly from what is presented herein due to ongoing updates and improvements by Google. We encourage you to explore the latest documentation and interface within Google AI Studio for the most up-to-date information.

By the end of this book, you'll not only understand the workings of Google AI Studio but also have the skills and knowledge to build your own AI applications. I invite you to join me on this journey and unlock the remarkable capabilities of artificial intelligence with Google AI Studio. Let's explore this amazing landscape together.

PREFACE

The world is witnessing a remarkable shift, propelled by the rapid advancements in artificial intelligence. AI is no longer a distant concept or a novelty, but a powerful technology that has reshaped our lives in countless ways. It is now a driving force behind innovations across various industries and fields, from automating mundane tasks to powering complex scientific research. Understanding and leveraging the potential of AI is becoming increasingly vital for navigating the modern era.

This book emerged from a desire to demystify the complexities of AI and make it accessible to everyone, regardless of their technical background. I believe that AI should be a tool for all, and Google AI Studio provides a unique opportunity for individuals, developers, researchers, and entrepreneurs to harness the capabilities of AI in creative and pragmatic ways. My aim is to provide you, the reader, with practical insights and hands-on experience that you can use to bring your innovative AI projects to life.

Google AI Studio is a sophisticated yet surprisingly user-friendly platform that puts AI capabilities directly into your hands. This book is designed to serve as a comprehensive guide, helping you navigate every aspect of this tool and explore its myriad possibilities. Whether you are taking your first steps into the world of AI or you are a developer looking to enhance your toolkit with AI technologies, this book aims to give you the solid foundation needed for success.

Throughout the book, you'll find in-depth explanations of key concepts, step-by-step tutorials, real-world case studies, and best practices that will empower you to not only understand but also implement AI. I invite you to embark on this journey with me and discover the limitless opportunities that Google AI Studio can offer. Let's together shape the future of AI-driven innovation.

CHAPTER 1:INTRODUCTION TO AI & GOOGLE AI STUDIO

What is Artificial Intelligence?

At its core, Artificial Intelligence (AI) is a computer system trained to recognize patterns and learn from vast amounts of data. Think of it like teaching a child: the more examples they see, the better they become at making predictions about new situations.

Example: Imagine showing a child hundreds of pictures of cats and dogs. After seeing enough examples, the child learns to identify the differences - cats have pointy ears, dogs often have longer snouts. Now when shown a new animal they've never seen before, they can guess correctly if it's a cat or dog based on these learned patterns.

That's how AI works - it learns from data and applies that knowledge to make intelligent decisions.

The Democratization of Magic: A Brief History of AI Accessibility

To truly understand the power of Google AI Studio today, we must first appreciate the staggering speed at which the barriers to entry have crumbled. In the span of half a decade, Artificial Intelligence has transformed from a scientific discipline reserved for the elite into a creative utility available to the masses.

2020: The Era of the Ivory Tower

The Barrier: Exclusivity

Just five years ago, "State-of-the-Art" AI was a walled garden. It was a discipline defined by scarcity and intense academic rigor.

- **The Gatekeepers:** Accessing high-level Large Language Models (LLMs) wasn't a matter of signing up; it was a matter of approval. You needed to be a researcher at a major university or an engineer at a tech giant.
- **The Cost:** Training and running these models required computational power that cost millions of dollars—massive server farms that were out of reach for anyone but the Fortune 500.
- **The Requirement:** If you didn't have a PhD in Machine Learning or advanced data science credentials, the door was effectively locked. AI was something you read about in sci-fi, not something you touched.

2023: The Era of the Mechanic

The Barrier: Complexity

By 2023, the walls had cracked. APIs (Application Programming Interfaces) had opened up, and the world saw the first wave of viral chatbots. But while you could *chat* with AI, **building** with it was still a messy, technical ordeal.

- **The "Glue" Code:** To create a custom AI workflow, you had to be a developer. You needed to know Python. You had to wrestle with API keys, manage rate limits, and write "spaghetti code" just to connect a prompt to a database.
- **The Friction:** It was powerful, but it wasn't user-friendly. You were like a mechanic working on an engine—your hands were constantly greasy with code, and if you didn't know how the gears turned, the machine wouldn't run.

2025: The Era of the Creator

The Barrier: Gone

Today, we have arrived at the moment of true democratization. Google AI Studio has fundamentally shifted the paradigm from *coding* to *creating*.

- **The New Syntax:** The requirement for Python or JavaScript has been replaced by natural language. If you can write a sentence, you can program a model.
- **Instant Access:** There are no waitlists and no million-dollar servers required. With a standard Google account, you have immediate access to Gemini 1.5 Pro and Flash—models more powerful than the supercomputers of 2020.
- **The Speed of Thought:** What used to take a team of engineers weeks to prototype can now be built, tested, and shared in the Playground in seconds. Technology has become invisible, leaving only the canvas for your ideas.

Google AI Studio represents a revolution in technology access. For the first time in history, an individual with just a computer and internet connection can harness the same AI power that major corporations use.

The Genesis of Google AI Studio: A Platform for AI Empowerment

At its core, Google AI Studio is a web-based platform designed to democratize artificial intelligence by making its complex mechanisms more accessible and user-friendly. It's a purpose-built environment for AI experimentation, development, and deployment, offering a seamless experience for both seasoned developers and beginners venturing into the world of AI for the first time. Unlike traditional AI development, which often requires extensive coding knowledge, specialized hardware, and a deep understanding of complex mathematical models, AI Studio streamlines the process by providing an intuitive interface that allows users to focus more on the creative aspects of AI rather than the technical intricacies.

The fundamental purpose behind Google AI Studio is to empower a diverse range of individuals and organizations to tap into the potential of AI without the need for a computer science degree. It's designed to be a sandbox for AI exploration, a playground for imaginative projects, and a launchpad for impactful AI applications. Whether your goal is to generate creative text, craft mesmerizing images, or prototype a sophisticated conversational chatbot, Google AI Studio offers the tools, resources, and support you need to begin building your AI-powered project immediately.

Unpacking the Benefits: Why Choose Google AI Studio?

The appeal of Google AI Studio stems from its numerous advantages over traditional AI development methods. Here are some of the key benefits that make it such a valuable and compelling platform:

•**Unparalleled Accessibility:** Perhaps the most significant benefit of Google AI Studio is its accessibility. Designed with a user-friendly interface and intuitive navigation, the platform welcomes users from all backgrounds and levels of experience. It provides a low barrier to entry for those curious about AI without prior knowledge, enabling them to start experimenting with the latest AI models quickly and easily.

•**Exceptional Ease of Use:** Gone are the days of painstakingly coding complex algorithms. With AI Studio, you don't need to be an expert in machine learning, nor a coding guru to bring your AI visions to life. The platform abstracts much of the complexity behind AI models, presenting users with straightforward interfaces and options, allowing you to focus on the creative and strategic aspects of your AI projects.

•**Rapid Prototyping Capabilities:** In the world of innovation, time is often of the essence. Google AI Studio enables rapid prototyping of AI applications with its high speed, efficient model deployment. With the platform's capability to allow immediate testing, iteration, and analysis, you can quickly see the results of your choices, enabling a faster, more iterative and experimental method.

•**Unparalleled Versatility:** Google AI Studio doesn't restrict you to just one type of AI application. It offers a suite of different AI models, enabling you to explore a wide range of use cases, from generating text-based content to creating stunning images, and everything in between. This versatility makes it an ideal platform for anyone exploring the breadth of AI possibilities.

•**Cost-Effectiveness:** Democratizing access to AI requires making it financially viable. Google AI Studio offers a free tier which allows users to experiment and prototype their applications. This cost-effectiveness opens doors for individuals, small businesses, and educational institutions to begin their AI journey without significant financial hurdles.

•**Seamless Google Ecosystem Integration:** Google AI Studio works flawlessly with other Google platforms, which can bring a lot of benefits to users already working with them. The platform has smooth integration with Google Cloud services such as Google Cloud Storage, Google Colab and more, which greatly enhances their functionality.

•**Comprehensive Learning Resources:** Beyond being just an AI tool, AI Studio also acts as an excellent learning resource by providing a range of educational materials. The platform also includes extensive documentation, hands-on guides, practical tutorials, and insightful examples, enabling users to learn and grow their AI skills at their own pace.

Meet Gemini: Google's AI Brain

Google AI Studio is powered by "Gemini," Google's most advanced AI model family. Think of Gemini like having multiple specialized tools:

 GEMINI 3 PRO PREVIEW
The Most Intelligent
- Best for: Complex reasoning, detailed analysis, coding
- Speed: Medium (5-30 seconds)
- Perfect for: When you need the best possible answer

 GEMINI FLASH
The Speed Demon
- Best for: Quick responses, general questions, chat
- Speed: Very Fast (1-5 seconds)
- Perfect for: When speed matters

 NANO BANANA PRO
Image Generation & Editing
- Best for: Creating and editing images
- Speed: Medium (10-30 seconds)
- Perfect for: Visual content creation

 IMAGEN 4

Advanced Image Creation
- Best for: Photorealistic, detailed images
- Speed: Medium (15-45 seconds)
- Perfect for: Professional image generation

⬛ VEO 2/3
Video Generation
- Best for: Creating videos from text
- Speed: Slower (30-120 seconds)
- Perfect for: Video production

⬛ GEMINI TEXT-TO-SPEECH
Audio Generation
- Best for: Converting text to natural voice
- Speed: Very Fast (1-3 seconds)
- Perfect for: Audio content and narration

Unleashing Potential: What Can You Build?

Google AI Studio is not merely a chatbot; it is a multimodal engine. "Multimodal" is the key industry term here—it means the AI doesn't just process text; it fluently speaks the languages of code, light, sound, and motion.

Here is how you can transform your workflow across four distinct domains:

1. The Wordsmith (Advanced Text & Code)

Gone are the days of writer's block. Whether you are crafting natural language or computer syntax, the AI acts as an infinite drafting engine.

- **Creative Writing:** Draft entire blog posts, script screenplays, or generate engaging social media hooks in seconds.
- **Technical Communication:** Turn bullet points into professional emails, proposals, or white papers.
- **The "Polyglot" Coder:** Write, debug, and document code in dozens of languages (Python, JavaScript, C++) simply by describing what the software should do.

2. The Multimedia Studio (Images, Video & Audio)

You no longer need a separate subscription for every media type. The Playground serves as a centralized creative suite.

- **Visual Imagination:** Use **Imagen** to generate thumbnails, storyboard concepts, or photorealistic assets for presentations.
- **Cinematic Production:** Utilize **Veo** to generate short video loops and backgrounds from text descriptions, perfect for social media or prototyping.
- **Sonic Branding:** Convert your written scripts into lifelike speech using **Gemini Audio**, ideal for voiceovers, accessibility features, or podcast intros.

3. The Analyst (Deep Reasoning & Vision)

This is Google's "Killer Feature." Thanks to Gemini's massive context window (the ability to "remember" huge amounts of data), you can upload files directly into the interface.

- **Visual Intelligence:** Upload a photo of a graph and ask the AI to extract the raw data into a spreadsheet. Upload a screenshot of a website and ask it to write the code to recreate it.
- **Document Mastery:** Upload a 500-page PDF, a contract, or a scientific paper and ask for specific summaries, citations, or simplified explanations.
- **Video Analysis:** Upload a video file and ask the AI to find the exact timestamp where a specific event happens (e.g., "At what second does the player score the goal?").

4. The Strategist (Business & Automation)

Move from raw data to actionable insights.

- **Market Simulation:** Roleplay negotiations or interview scenarios to prepare for high-stakes meetings.
- **Data Synthesis:** Feed the model disparate reports and ask it to identify trends, anomalies, or opportunities that a human might miss.
- **Rapid Prototyping:** Sketch a business idea on a napkin, take a picture, and ask the AI to generate a business plan, a marketing tagline, and a landing page structure.

5.Build the app

In this ecosystem, English is the new programming language. If you can describe your idea clearly, you can build a functional application. Ai studio can also do the process of "No-Code" development, where you act as the **Product Manager** and Gemini acts as your **Lead Engineer**.

The Bottom Line

Google AI Studio grants you access to a "Staff on Demand"—a writer, an artist, a coder, and a data scientist—all waiting for your instructions in a single interface. What was once the proprietary advantage of Fortune 500 tech giants is now a free utility available to you.

Who Should Use Google AI Studio?

Google AI Studio is designed to be versatile and cater to a broad spectrum of users, each with their own unique interests and goals:

- *AI Beginners:* Individuals new to the field of AI will find Google AI Studio to be an ideal platform to understand and engage with the technology. This tool allows you to explore the possibilities of AI in a user-friendly setting.
- *Experienced Developers:* Seasoned developers can leverage AI Studio for its rapid prototyping capabilities and the smooth integration of AI components into other applications. The

platform's adaptability and scalability make it perfect for developers to streamline their workflows and deliver new AI driven solutions.

- *Researchers:* Researchers working in the field of AI will find Google AI Studio a valuable resource for quickly testing their hypotheses and developing new AI models. The platform's accessibility to multiple AI models enable quick experimentation and iterative research.

- *Educators:* Google AI Studio is ideal for educators looking to integrate AI into their curricula by providing a hands-on experience to their students. This tool allows students to develop and experiment with AI without the high barriers of entry that usually comes with these technologies.

- *Entrepreneurs and Startups:* For startups and small businesses, AI Studio offers a cost-effective platform to bring their innovative AI ideas to life, develop prototypes, and validate their concepts, all without requiring significant financial investment in computational resources.

- *Creative Content Creators:* Artists, authors, designers, and other creative professionals can use AI Studio to explore innovative ways to enhance their work. Google AI Studio acts as a tool to spark inspiration, create unique content, and refine existing projects.

You don't need to be tech-savvy or have any AI background. Google AI Studio is designed for beginners!

In conclusion, Google AI Studio is not merely a tool; it's a catalyst for innovation and a gateway to the transformative potential of AI. It is a powerful, user-friendly, and constantly evolving platform that enables all individuals to explore, create and build the AI driven applications of tomorrow.

This book has been prepared with the information available up to its publication date. Please be aware that Google AI Studio is a continuously evolving platform. Therefore, some features, functionalities, and menu names may differ slightly from what is presented herein due to ongoing updates and improvements by Google. We encourage you to explore the latest documentation and interface within Google AI Studio for the most up-to-date information.

CHAPTER 2:GETTING STARTED - YOUR FIRST LOGIN

Before we can build the future, we must enter the laboratory. Accessing Google AI Studio is designed to be frictionless. There are no software downloads, no installation wizards, and no credit cards required to start.

All you need is a your Google Account—and a web browser.

Creating a Google Account

Google AI Studio relies on the robust security infrastructure of the Google ecosystem. If you already use Gmail, Google Drive, or YouTube, you already have the key.

If you do not have a Google Account, follow these steps to mint one:

1. **Navigate:** Open your browser and visit https://accounts.google.com/signup.
2. **Identify:** Enter your **First** and **Last Name**.
3. **Choose Your Handle:** Create a unique username (this will be your @gmail.com address).
4. **Secure:** Choose a password that mixes complexity with memorability.
5. **Verify:** Google requires a mobile phone number to prevent spam. Enter your number and type the 6-digit code sent to you via SMS.

6. **Finalize:** Agree to the Terms of Service.

Accessing Google AI Studio

Once your account is active, entering the studio is a matter of seconds.:

STEP 1: Open Your Browser
Use any modern browser (Chrome, Firefox, Safari, Edge)

STEP 2: Go to Google AI Studio
Type or paste this URL in the address bar:
https://aistudio.google.com

STEP 3: If you are not already logged into your browser, you will see the standard Google Sign-In prompt.

- Enter your **Email Address**.
- Enter your **Password**.
- *Note:* If you have 2-Step Verification enabled (highly recommended), approve the login via your phone or security key.

STEP 4: Grant Permissions
- Google AI Studio asks for access to your account
- Click "Allow" or "Continue"
- You'll be redirected to Google AI Studio

Voilà! You're now inside Google AI Studio!

Your First Look at the Dashboard

When you first open Google AI Studio, you'll see:

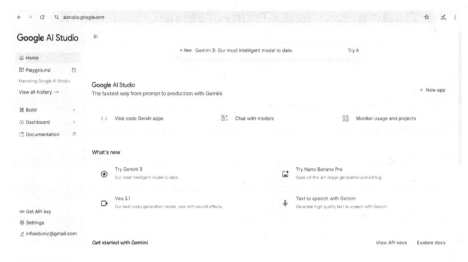

TOP BAR:
- Google AI Studio logo (click to go home)
- Navigation buttons
- Your account menu (top right)

MAIN AREA:
- "What's New" announcement banner
- Featured AI models
- Quick start options
- Links to help and documentation

LEFT SIDEBAR (if visible):
- Home
- Playground
- Build
- Dashboard
- Documentation
- Settings

Understanding Your Free Plan

Google AI Studio offers a generous FREE tier:

✓ TEXT GENERATION
- Unlimited requests with rate limits
- Use all Gemini text models
- Generate as much text as you want

✓ IMAGE GENERATION
- ~25 free images per day
- Using Imagen 4 or Nano Banana Pro
- After free quota, upgrade for more

✓ TEXT-TO-SPEECH
- Free speech generation
- Multiple voice options
- No daily limit

✓ PREMIUM FEATURES
- Video generation (requires paid plan)
- Higher rate limits (with paid upgrade)

You can use Google AI Studio extensively with just the free tier!

Quick Tour of Key Sections

Take 5 minutes to explore:

• Click "Playground" to see where you'll work most
• Click "Build" to see app-building tools
• Click "Dashboard" to see your usage and projects
• Click Settings icon (gear) to adjust preferences

Common First-Time Questions

Q: Do I need to pay anything to start?
A: No! The free tier is very generous. No payment info required to start.

Q: Is my information safe?
A: Yes! Google uses enterprise-grade security and encryption. Your data is safe.

Q: Can I use it on my phone?
A: It works on mobile, but the experience is best on a computer or tablet.

Q: What if I made a mistake during signup?
A: Most information can be changed in Account Settings.

Q: Can I delete my account later?
A: Yes, you can delete your Google account anytime from Settings.

You're now officially set up! You're ready to create your first AI prompt.

CHAPTER 3:MASTERING THE UNIFIED PLAYGROUND IN GOOGLE AI STUDIO

Google AI Studio has reimagined the developer experience with a unified **Playground**. This evolution moves away from fragmented prompt types, consolidating them into a single, streamlined interface. Whether you are prototyping a simple chatbot, testing complex reasoning, or generating multimedia assets, the Playground is now your central hub.

This chapter serves as a comprehensive guide to navigating, configuring, and mastering this interactive workspace.

The Playground is Your Canvas

Think of the Playground as a fusion between a sophisticated text editor and a modern chat application. It is designed for rapid iteration, allowing you to:

- **Draft Prompts:** Input natural language requests or structured instructions.
- **Visualize Responses:** View real-time output from the model.
- **Fine-tune Parameters:** Adjust creativity, safety, and formatting on the fly.
- **Manage Assets:** Seamlessly integrate text, images, and media.

Think of it like a text editor combined with a chat application.

The Playground Layout

The Playground is divided into three logical zones to optimize your workflow:

1. **Top Navigation (Model Selection):** The command center for choosing your AI model.
2. **Middle Workspace (Settings & Tools):** Where you configure model behavior and manage the session.
3. **Bottom Zone (Interaction):** The input/output loop where the conversation happens.

TOP SECTION - MODEL SELECTION:

- Shows available AI models in a carousel
- "Featured" tab - Recommended models
- "Gemini" tab - Text/conversation models
- "Live" tab - Real-time input models
- "Images" tab - Image generation models
- "Video" tab - Video generation
- "Audio" tab - Text-to-speech models

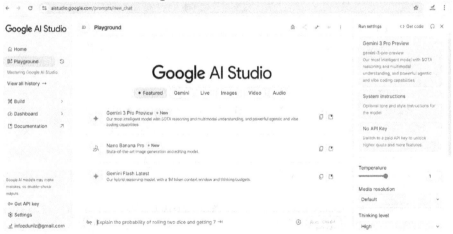

You click any model to select it and start using it.

MIDDLE SECTION - SETTINGS AREA:
- Settings gear icon (top right) for advanced options
- Share button to share your work
- "New chat" button to start fresh
- More options menu (...)

BOTTOM SECTION - INPUT & OUTPUT:
- Large text field for typing your prompt
- Asset button to add files, images, or audio
- "Run" button (or Ctrl+Enter) to execute your prompt
- Conversation history showing your messages and AI responses

The Model Carousel Explained

When you first enter the Playground, the most prominent feature is the **Model Carousel**. This row of cards represents the available intelligence engines you can harness.

To help you find the right tool for the job, models are organized into intuitive tabs:

- **Featured:** A curated selection of the most capable and popular models (e.g., high-performance reasoning models).
- **Gemini:** Dedicated to Google's flagship text and conversation models (e.g., Gemini 3 Pro, Flash).
- **Live:** Optimized models for real-time, low-latency input requirements.
- **Images:** Specialized models for generating or analyzing visual content.
- **Video:** Models capable of video generation or multimodal understanding.
- **Audio:** Text-to-speech and audio processing models.

How to Select: simply click on a model card (e.g., "Gemini 3 Pro Preview"). The card displays essential metadata, including a brief description of capabilities and a "New" badge for recently released versions.

When you first open the Playground, you see the MODEL

CAROUSEL - rows of available AI models.

Each model shows:
- Model name (e.g., "Gemini 3 Pro Preview")
- A description of what it does
- A "New" badge if it's newly released
- Copy button to copy its name
- Link to official documentation

Simply click on a model card to select it.

Fine-Tuning Intelligence: The Settings Menu

The true power of Google AI Studio lies in its configurability. Located in the top-right (Gear Icon), the Settings menu allows you to shape how the AI "thinks" and responds.

Core Configuration Options

Model Selection

Even after selecting a model from the carousel, you can quickly swap between versions (e.g., switching from *Pro* to *Flash* to test speed versus quality) directly within this menu.

Creativity Slider (Temperature)

This control determines the "randomness" of the output:

- **Low (0):** Deterministic, factual, and precise. Ideal for coding, math, or data extraction.
- **Balanced (1):** The default setting. A healthy mix of accuracy and fluency.
- **High (2):** Creative, imaginative, and diverse. Best for brainstorming, poetry, or fiction writing.

Response Length

Control the verbosity of the AI's output:

- **Short:** 1–2 sentences (concise answers).
- **Medium:** 2–4 paragraphs (standard explanations).
- **Long:** 4+ paragraphs (comprehensive articles or reports).

Output Format

Define the structure of the response to fit your application's needs:

- **Plain Text:** Standard natural language.
- **JSON:** Returns structured data, essential for programmatically parsing responses in apps.
- **Markdown:** Returns text with formatting (headers, lists, bolding).
- **Code:** returns raw code with syntax highlighting.

Safety Settings

Responsible AI controls allow you to filter content based on appropriateness. While the default settings are tuned for general safety, you can adjust these thresholds based on your use case requirements.

The Conversation Area

The heart of the Playground is the conversation view. This is where you communicate with the model.

Inputting Data

- **Text Field:** A large, expansive area for typing complex prompts.
- **Multimodal Assets:** Click the **(+) Asset button** to upload files, images, or audio clips. This allows you to perform tasks like "Describe this image" or "Summarize this audio file."

- **Execution:** Press the **Run** button (or use the shortcut `Ctrl +Enter`) to send your request.

Analyzing the Output

Each interaction is clearly labeled:

- **USER:** Your input (text + assets).
- **MODEL:** The AI's generation.

Key Metrics & Tools:

- **Token Count:** Visible for every exchange, helping you monitor resource usage and cost.
- **Feedback:** Use the Thumbs Up/Down icons to help improve model performance.
- **Copy Response:** A one-click button to copy the AI's text to your clipboard.

Navigation & Project Management: The Sidebar

Access the global navigation menu by clicking the **Hamburger icon (≡)** in the top left. This sidebar connects the Playground to the broader ecosystem of Google AI Studio.

- **HOME:** Your landing page. View "What's New" updates and access your recent projects quickly.
- **PLAYGROUND:** Returns you to your current active workspace.
- **BUILD:** The deployment hub. Browse the app gallery, save your prompt as an app, or deploy it to production.
- **DASHBOARD:** The administrative center. Here you can manage API keys, monitor your token usage, and view billing details.
- **DOCUMENTATION:** Direct links to official guides, API references, and deep-dive tutorials.
- **SETTINGS:** Global account preferences, privacy controls, and interface defaults.

The unified Playground in Google AI Studio removes the friction between having an idea and testing it. By mastering the **Model**

Carousel, utilizing **Settings** to control output, and leveraging the multimodal **Conversation Area**, you can move from simple prompting to building robust AI applications with ease.

CHAPTER 4: CREATING YOUR FIRST TEXT PROMPT

What is a Prompt?

A "prompt" is your request or instruction to the AI. It's like asking a question or giving a command.

Examples of prompts:
- "Write a professional email to my boss"
- "Explain quantum physics in simple terms"
- "Generate 5 ideas for social media posts"
- "Debug this Python code"
- "Create a product description for a blue notebook"

The better your prompt, the better your response!

Your First Prompt: Step-by-Step

STEP 1: Go to Playground
- Click "Playground" in the sidebar
- You'll see the model carousel

STEP 2: Choose a Model
- For text, click "Gemini 3 Pro Preview" or "Gemini Flash"

- A confirmation appears

STEP 3: Write Your Prompt
- Click in the text field at the bottom
- Type a simple request

Example prompt:
"Tell me 3 benefits of learning Python programming"

STEP 4: Execute Your Prompt
- Click the "Run" button
- OR press Ctrl+Enter
- Wait 2-10 seconds

STEP 5: See the Response
- Your prompt appears with "USER" label
- The AI response appears with "MODEL" label
- The response includes token usage

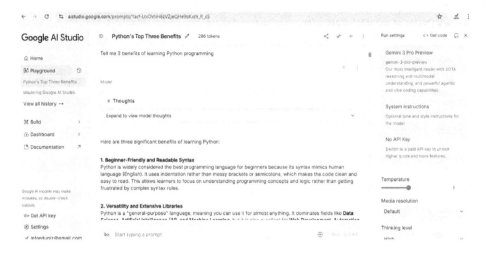

Tips for Better Prompts

BE SPECIFIC:
☐ Bad: "Write something about AI"
✓ Good: "Write a 300-word article about how AI is transforming healthcare"

GIVE CONTEXT:
☐ Bad: "Explain this"
✓ Good: "Explain blockchain technology for someone with no technical background"

SPECIFY FORMAT:
☐ Bad: "Give me ideas"
✓ Good: "Give me 5 social media post ideas in bullet format"

SET CONSTRAINTS:
☐ Bad: "Write something"
✓ Good: "Write a 100-word product description"

Example Prompts to Try

TRY THESE TO LEARN:

Prompt 1 - Learning:
"Explain how photosynthesis works in a way a 10-year-old could understand"

Prompt 2 - Brainstorming:
"Give me 10 creative ideas for a YouTube channel about personal productivity"

Prompt 3 - Writing:
"Write a professional job application cover letter for a Marketing Manager position"

Prompt 4 - Analysis:
"What are the pros and cons of working from home?"

Prompt 5 - Code:
"Write Python code to calculate the factorial of a number"

Understanding the Response

When you receive a response, you'll see:

TOKEN COUNT:
- Shows how many "tokens" were used
- Tokens are roughly 4 characters each
- More tokens = longer response
- Helps track your usage

FEEDBACK BUTTONS:
- Thumbs up (☐) - Response was helpful
- Thumbs down (☐) - Response could be better
- Your feedback helps Google improve

COPY BUTTON:
- Copy the response to clipboard
- Paste it anywhere you want

The Psychology of Effective Prompts

Understanding how to write prompts that generate the results you want is one of the most valuable skills in the AI era. Effective prompting isn't magic—it's a combination of clarity, context, and strategic communication.

Key Principles of Advanced Prompting:

Prompt engineering, at its core, is the art of designing specific, clear, and well-structured instructions for the AI model. It's about framing your requests in a way that guides the model toward the most accurate and relevant response. Think of it like giving very specific directions – the better the directions, the easier it is to arrive at the destination.

1. Specificity and Context
The more specific your prompt, the better the AI can understand your needs. Instead of asking "Write me something about Google AI Studio," try "Write a 500-word beginner's guide explaining what Google AI Studio is, its main features including text, image, video, and audio generation, and why someone with no AI experience should use it."

Context matters tremendously. If you're generating content for a specific audience, include that. For example: "Write a friendly, conversational tutorial for a 10-year-old explaining how to create AI artwork using Google AI Studio."

2. Role and Perspective Assignment
Assigning a role to the AI can dramatically improve results. Examples:
- "Act as a professional software trainer and explain..."
- "You are a creative writing expert. Please help me..."
- "As a business consultant, what would you recommend..."

3. Output Format Specification
Be explicit about the format you want:
- "Provide your response as a numbered list"
- "Format this as a step-by-step tutorial with code examples"
- "Create a table comparing..."
- "Write this as a dialogue between two people"

4. Iterative Refinement
Rarely do you get perfect results on the first attempt. Use follow-up prompts to refine:
- "Can you make that more formal/casual?"
- "Expand on the third point"
- "Combine these two responses and eliminate repetition"
- "Simplify the technical jargon"

Advanced Text Generation Strategies

Beyond simple text generation, Gemini can handle complex writing tasks:

Content Repurposing: Input one piece of content and get multiple outputs:
- Blog post → Tweet thread → LinkedIn article → Video script
- Research paper → Executive summary → Social media post
- Product description → FAQ → Customer testimonial angles

Tone and Style Adaptation: Ask Gemini to rewrite content in different styles:
- Same content written for different audiences (5-year-old, teenager, adult professional)
- Different tones: humorous, serious, motivational, technical
- Different formats: formal report, casual blog post, social media post

Language and Localization:

- "Translate this to Spanish and adapt cultural references appropriately"
- "Rewrite this for a British English audience"
- "Make this funny for an Australian audience"

Real-World Writing Projects

Example 1: Business Email Drafting
Prompt: "I need to send a professional but friendly email to a client who is upset about a delayed project. The project was delayed due to circumstances beyond our control, and I want to apologize, explain briefly, and propose how we'll make it right."

Example 2: Creative Writing
Prompt: "Write a 1000-word short story in the style of science fiction. The setting is a futuristic city where AI has become conscious. The protagonist discovers something surprising about the AI's true nature."

Example 3: Educational Content
Prompt: "Create a comprehensive study guide for high school biology covering cell structure and function. Include:
- Clear explanations of each organelle
- Analogies to real-world objects
- Key vocabulary with definitions
- Practice questions with answers
- A summary diagram description"

Prompting for Different Model Strengths

Gemini 3 Pro Preview: Best for complex reasoning
Use for: Complex analysis, multi-step problem solving, research summaries
Example: "Analyze the pros and cons of remote work versus office work, considering impact on employee productivity, mental

health, and company culture."

Nano Banana Pro: Best for quick, efficient responses
Use for: Quick facts, simple questions, concise answers
Example: "What are the top 5 benefits of regular exercise?"

Nano Banana: Best for mobile and lightweight tasks
Use for: Mobile apps, simple classifications, basic Q&A
Example: "Is this sentence positive or negative? 'The weather is beautiful today.'"

You now know the basics! Go ahead and experiment with your first prompt!

CHAPTER 5: TEXT GENERATION & CONTENT CREATION

The Power of Gemini for Text

At its core, Gemini is a masterful manipulator of language. It does not simply "output text"; it adapts its persona, tone, and vocabulary to suit the specific architecture of your request. Whether you need the precision of a lawyer or the flair of a novelist, the model shifts gears instantly.

Here is how Gemini transforms your textual workflow:

1. The Editor-in-Chief (Content & Publishing)

Gemini excels at structuring long-form content that engages readers.

- **Articles & Blog Posts:** distinct ability to draft SEO-friendly headlines, structure logical arguments, and maintain a consistent voice throughout long pieces.
- **Creative Writing:** From short stories to screenplays, it can brainstorm plot twists, develop character backstories, and overcome writer's block.

2. The Corporate Communication Strategist

Eliminate the fatigue of "business speak." Gemini drafts professional correspondence with the perfect level of formality.

- **Emails & Letters:** Instantly generate polite refusals,

persuasive sales outreach, or formal internal memos.
- **Marketing Copy:** Create punchy slogans, compelling product descriptions, and ad copy tailored to specific demographics.

3. The Lead Engineer (Code & Technical Writing)

Gemini is trained on a massive dataset of public code repositories, making it one of the world's most capable coding assistants.

- **Code Generation:** Write functional scripts in Python, JavaScript, C++, and more.
- **Technical Documentation:** It doesn't just write the code; it writes the manual. Ask it to generate comments, API documentation, or "README" files for your projects.

4. The Data Analyst (Summarization & Insight)

This is Gemini's superpower. Thanks to its massive "Context Window," it can read more data at once than almost any other AI.

- **Deep Summarization:** Upload a 100-page PDF or a transcript of an hour-long meeting, and Gemini can extract the key bullet points, action items, and decisions.
- **Complex Analysis:** It can synthesize information from multiple documents to find contradictions, trends, or connections.

Practical Writing Prompts

Let's practice with real examples:

EXAMPLE 1 - Blog Post:
"Write a 500-word blog post about 5 productivity tips for remote workers. Use an engaging tone and include practical examples."

EXAMPLE 2 - Email:
"Draft a professional email to a client explaining why their project deadline needs to be extended by 2 weeks. Be polite but firm."

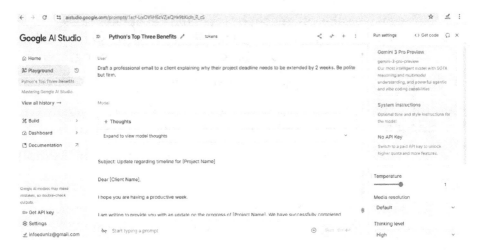

EXAMPLE 3 - Social Media:
"Create 5 Instagram post captions about healthy eating. Make them engaging, use relevant emojis, and include a call-to-action."

EXAMPLE 4 - Product Description:
"Write an Amazon product description for a noise-canceling wireless headphone. Include features, benefits, and why customers should buy it."

EXAMPLE 5 - Code:
"Write JavaScript code that fetches data from an API and displays it in an HTML table. Include error handling."

Advanced Text Features

GEMINI 3 PRO EXTENDED THINKING:
Gemini 3 Pro can "think through" complex problems:
- Click settings
- Enable "Extended Thinking"
- AI shows its reasoning process
- Better for complex analysis

TONE AND STYLE:
Specify the tone in your prompt:
- "Write in a casual, friendly tone"

- "Write in a professional, formal tone"
- "Write like you're explaining to a friend"
- "Write in an academic tone"

LENGTH CONTROL:
- "Write approximately 300 words"
- "Keep it to 2 paragraphs"
- "Make it concise - under 100 words"

Tips for Getting Better Content

INCLUDE EXAMPLES:
"Write a how-to guide on making homemade pasta.
Example tone: Use an enthusiastic, encouraging tone like a cooking instructor.
Example structure: Start with ingredients, then step-by-step instructions, finish with tips."

GIVE TARGET AUDIENCE:
"Write a product review of an iPhone 15.
Target audience: College students (tech-savvy, price-conscious)
Format: 300-400 words, includes pros/cons"

SPECIFY OUTPUT FORMAT:
"Create 5 email subject lines for a product launch.
Format: Numbered list
Include: Why each subject line is effective"

Editing and Iterating

If the response isn't quite right:

FOLLOW UP WITH:
- "Can you make this more concise?"
- "Add more examples to this"
- "Rewrite in a more casual tone"
- "Make this more persuasive"

- "Add statistics to support these points"

REFINE THE ORIGINAL:
- Save the response you liked
- Adjust one element in your new prompt
- Run again to compare

COMBINE RESPONSES:
- Generate multiple versions
- Copy the best parts from each
- Combine into your final version

Real-World Text Generation Workflow

Here's how professionals use it:

1. BRAINSTORM:
"Generate 10 blog post topics about digital marketing for 2025"

2. OUTLINE:
"Create a detailed outline for a blog post about SEO best practices"

3. DRAFT:
"Write a 1000-word blog post from this outline: [paste outline]"

4. ENHANCE:

"Add keywords to optimize this for SEO: [paste draft]"

5. POLISH:
"Proofread and improve this text for readability: [paste draft]"

6. EXPORT:
Copy final version and paste into your publishing platform

Writing Prompts You Can Try Now

✓ "Explain cryptocurrency to my grandmother"
✓ "Write 5 funny pickup lines (clean, appropriate for all ages)"
✓ "Create a detailed recipe for chocolate chip cookies"
✓ "Write a professional cover letter for a [JOB] position at [COMPANY]"
✓ "Summarize this news article in 3 bullet points: [ARTICLE TEXT]"
✓ "Generate 10 business name ideas for a sustainable fashion brand"
✓ "Write a thank you email to a mentor"
✓ "Create a travel itinerary for a 5-day trip to [CITY]"

Text generation is the foundation of Google AI Studio. Master it and you'll unlock endless possibilities!

CHAPTER 6: IMAGE GENERATION

What is Image Generation?

Image generation means creating pictures from text descriptions using AI. You describe what you want, and the AI creates a visual image.

Now, we'll delve deeper into how to leverage the Gemini model within Google AI Studio to understand, analyze, and extract information from images. It's crucial to note that while the Gemini model doesn't directly generate images, its image analysis capabilities can be incredibly powerful, and we can integrate these with external tools to create a full image-based workflow. You'll learn how to upload images, craft prompts that extract valuable information, and explore various image analysis techniques available through the model. By the end of this chapter, you'll be able to leverage Google AI Studio to understand and analyze images, unlocking new possibilities for creative and analytical projects.

Examples:
- "A sunset over a calm lake with mountains in the background"
- "A modern minimalist living room with blue sofa and plants"
- "A cartoon character of a friendly robot made of copper and gears"
- "A professional headshot of a woman in business attire"
- "A futuristic city with flying cars and neon lights"

Choosing Between Image Models

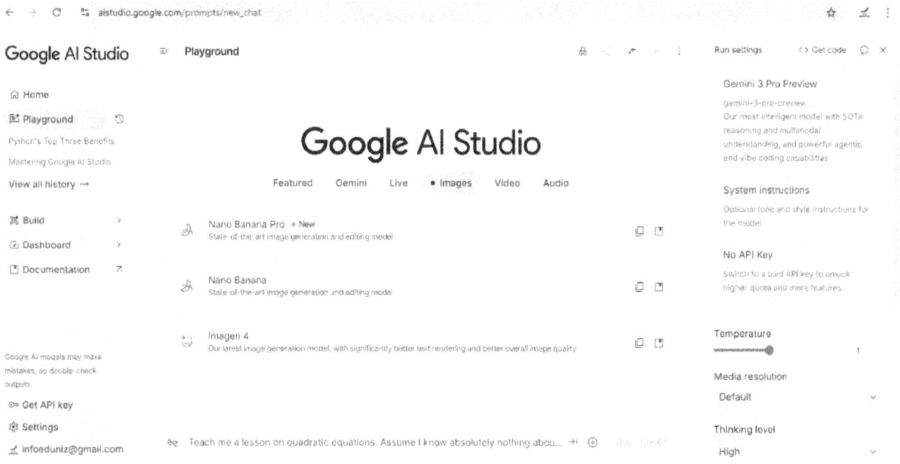

This screenshot displays the Images tab within Google AI Studio, showing available image generation models:

- Nano Banana Pro (New) - described as state-of-the-art image generation and editing model
- Nano Banana - state-of-the-art image generation and editing model
- Imagen 4 - our latest image generation model with significantly better text rendering and overall image quality

The interface clearly displays each model with its description, allowing users to easily understand the capabilities and differences between the available image generation options.

NANO BANANA PRO:latest model till November 2025
- Speed: Medium
- Best for: General image creation and editing
- Can edit existing images
- Good quality
- Great for most uses

IMAGEN 4:
- Speed: Medium (15-45 seconds)
- Best for: Photorealistic, detailed images
- Professional quality
- Better text rendering in images
- Premium results
- Ideal for high-stakes projects

Step-by-Step: Create Your First Image

STEP 1: Go to Playground
- Click "Playground" in sidebar

STEP 2: Click "Images" Tab
- You'll see image generation models

STEP 3: Select a Model
- Click "Imagen 4" or "Nano Banana"
- Confirmation appears

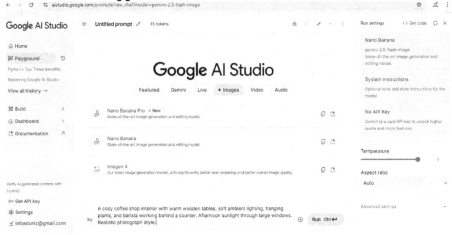

STEP 4: Write Your Prompt
- Click the "Describe your image" field
- Type a detailed description

Example:
"A cozy coffee shop interior with warm wooden tables, soft ambient lighting, hanging plants, and barista working behind a counter. Afternoon sunlight through large windows. Realistic photograph style."

STEP 5: Click "Run"
- Wait 15-45 seconds
- Image appears in gallery

STEP 6: Download or Use
- Right-click to download
- Copy to clipboard
- Use in documents or projects

Tips for Getting the Best Results

- **Prompt Engineering is Key:** The better you can write prompts, the better your images.
- **Experiment with Parameters:** Play around with the different settings and options available in Google AI Studio. See how they affect the generated image.
- **Iterate and Refine:** Don't be afraid to generate multiple images and refine your prompts based on the results. Image

generation is an iterative process.
- **Check the Terms of Service:** Be aware of any usage restrictions or guidelines related to the generated images.
- **Safety First:** Ensure you're following the guidelines from Google on ensuring the safety of Generative AI.

The Art of AI Image Prompting

Generating images with AI requires a different mindset than text prompting. Success comes from:

1. Visual Vocabulary
Learn to describe visual elements precisely:
- Color: "Vibrant sunset orange" vs "Orange"
- Style: "Photorealistic" vs "Impressionist painting" vs "Anime style"
- Composition: "Wide-angle perspective" vs "Close-up" vs "Aerial view"
- Lighting: "Golden hour sunlight" vs "Harsh shadows" vs "Soft diffused light"
- Mood: "Serene and peaceful" vs "Chaotic and energetic"

2. Detailed Element Specification
Include specific details:
- "A woman with curly auburn hair, wearing a green sweater, smiling, sitting in a coffee shop with warm lighting"
- Rather than: "A woman in a coffee shop"

3. Technical Parameters
- Resolution: "High resolution" vs "8K quality"
- Aspect ratio: "16:9 landscape" vs "Square 1:1" vs "9:16 portrait"
- Style reference: "In the style of Van Gogh" or "Like a movie poster" or "Album cover aesthetic"

GOOD PROMPTS INCLUDE:

SUBJECT:

What is the main focus?
"A golden retriever puppy"

SETTING:
Where is it located?
"...playing on a beach at sunset"

STYLE:
What artistic style?
"...in a watercolor painting style"

MOOD:
What feeling?
"...with warm, happy lighting"

QUALITY:
How detailed?
"...highly detailed, professional photograph"

FULL EXAMPLE:
"A cozy wooden cabin in snowy mountains at night, warm light glowing from windows, smoke from chimney, Christmas decorations, professional photography, highly detailed, winter atmosphere"

Pro Tips for Better Images

✓ BE SPECIFIC - The more detail, the better
✓ USE DESCRIPTIVE ADJECTIVES - "golden", "misty", "vibrant", "soft"
✓ MENTION STYLE - "oil painting", "photograph", "digital art", "sketch"
✓ SPECIFY LIGHTING - "golden hour", "dramatic shadows", "bright sunlight"
✓ INCLUDE CAMERA DETAILS - "wide angle", "macro photography", "portrait mode"

✓ MENTION MOOD - "peaceful", "energetic", "mysterious", "cheerful"

Image Generation Prompts to Try

✓ "A minimalist desk workspace with Mac computer, coffee cup, plants, and notebook. Bright natural light. Clean, professional photograph."
✓ "An underwater ocean scene with colorful coral reef, tropical fish, rays of sunlight from above. Realistic illustration."
✓ "A futuristic robot standing in a neon city at night. Cyberpunk style. Highly detailed."
✓ "A rustic farmhouse kitchen with vintage appliances, wooden counter, and flowers in a vase. Cozy warm lighting. Magazine photography style."
✓ "A magical forest with glowing trees, floating orbs of light, and a mystical pathway. Fantasy art style."

Image Editing with Nano Banana or Nano Banana Pro

Nano Banana can edit existing images:

1. Upload an image
2. Describe what you want to change
3. AI modifies the image

Examples:
- "Change the sky to sunset colors"
- "Remove the person from the background"
- "Make the colors more vibrant"
- "Change the season from summer to winter"

Practical Use Cases

SOCIAL MEDIA:
- Generate custom thumbnails
- Create branded graphics
- Design post covers
- Make eye-catching visuals

BLOGS & WEBSITES:
- Generate hero images
- Create featured images
- Design illustrations
- Add visual content

MARKETING:
- Create product mockups
- Generate lifestyle images
- Design promotional graphics
- Visualize concepts

CREATIVE PROJECTS:
- Illustrate stories
- Design concept art
- Create character visuals

- Prototype ideas

Important Notes

▢ LIMITATIONS:
- May refuse inappropriate requests
- Quality depends on prompt clarity
- Different runs may give different results

✓ BENEFITS:
- Instant visual content
- No design skills needed
- Royalty-free images
- Unique, custom visuals
- Quick iteration

Image generation opens creative possibilities for everyone!

CHAPTER 7: VIDEO GENERATION

You've mastered generating creative text and compelling static images. Now, let's add the dimension of time and motion! Google AI Studio is continuously evolving, and it now offers the exciting ability to generate dynamic video clips directly from your text prompts. This capability allows you to bring your ideas to life in a whole new way, creating short scenes and visual concepts. This chapter will guide you through accessing the video generation tool, understanding the model that powers it, crafting prompts for motion, and generating your first video clips. Be aware that this feature, like many advanced AI tools, may have introductory usage limits.

7.1 Introduction to AI Video Generation

This interface demonstrates the video generation capabilities available in Google AI Studio, making it clear that Veo 2 is the primary tool for creating video content through AI.

Note: The name of the model may evolve or change as the technology is updated. Confirming the name in your UI is the most accurate way to know.

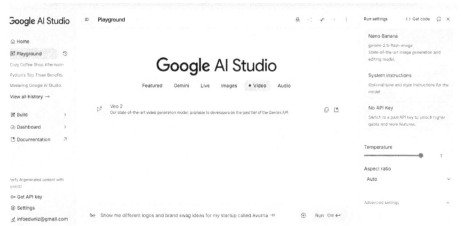

This screenshot showcases the Video tab in Google AI Studio, featuring:
- Veo 2 (marked as the latest video generation model till November 2025 in free tier)

Veo is Google's advanced video generation model that creates moving scenes from text descriptions.

What Veo Can Do:
- Generate short videos
- Create realistic animations
- Produce different visual styles
- Generate consistent scenes
- Create story sequences

Video Generation Basics

When you use Veo, you:
1. Write a detailed description
2. Specify the visual style
3. Set video length
4. Click Run
5. Wait 30-120 seconds
6. Download your video

Writing Video Prompts

Writing prompts for video requires a different mindset than for text or even static images. You need to describe action, transitions, and the progression of events over time.

- Key Elements for Video Prompts:
  Subject(s) and Actions: Clearly state who or what is in the video and what they are doing. Use action verbs! (e.g., "A person is walking," "Birds are flying," "The water flows").
  Setting/Environment: Describe where the action is happening. Be specific about the location and its features. (e.g., "in a bustling city square," "on a calm forest path," "above the

clouds").

Style and Mood: Convey the desired visual aesthetic and emotional tone. (e.g., "cinematic," "dreamy," "gritty," "colorful animation").

Implied Camera Movement (Optional but helpful): While direct camera controls might be limited, describing the perspective can sometimes influence the output (e.g., "close-up of..." "wide shot of...").

Progression/Simple Sequence: For slightly longer clips, you might hint at a simple sequence of events if the duration allows.BEST VIDEO PROMPTS INCLUDE:

ACTION:
What's happening?
"A person jogging through a park"

CAMERA MOVEMENT:
How does the camera move?
"...with smooth tracking shots"

STYLE:
What's the visual style?
"...in cinematic photography style"

SETTING:
Where is it?
"...during golden hour"

MOOD:
What's the feeling?
"...peaceful and serene"

FULL EXAMPLE:
"A woman walking through a modern minimalist cafe, picking up a coffee, smiling at the camera. Smooth tracking shot. Bright natural light from windows. Realistic cinematic photography. Coffee shop setting."

Understanding Video Generation Parameters

•**Controlling the Output**: The video generation interface provides parameters to fine-tune your results. These will vary but commonly include:

Duration: This sets the length of the video clip, typically in seconds. Video generation is computationally intensive, so clips are often limited to a few seconds (e.g., 4-6 seconds).

Aspect Ratio: Choose the video's dimensions, such as Widescreen (16:9) or Vertical (9:16), depending on where you plan to use the video.

Negative keywords: It offers negative words which you want that should not be in video,you can define them in this section.

No.of Results (If Available): If you get more than one result you can change it from this section depending upon availability.

Resolution: You can change the resolution of the video in coming plans or paid plans.

Video Generation Prompts to Try

✓ "A person dancing to upbeat music in a modern living room. Smooth camera movement. Bright, energetic lighting. Music video style."

✓ "A scenic montage of a hiking trail through mountains.

Sunrise lighting. Smooth aerial drone shots. Different landscapes. Documentary style."

✓ "A busy coffee shop scene with people ordering, sitting, and chatting. Busy atmosphere. Multiple customers are visible. Realistic cinema style."

✓ "A product demo: A smartphone being rotated to show design. White background. Professional lighting. Commercial advertisement style."

✓ "A sunset time-lapse over an ocean beach. Colors changing from orange to purple. Waves gently rolling. Cinematic time-lapse."

Tips for Effective Video Prompts and Current Limitations

- Tips for Better Video:
  - o Focus on Action: Describe what is moving or happening.
  - o Be Descriptive: Use strong adjectives and adverbs to set the scene and mood.
  - o Keep it Simple (Initially): Start with straightforward concepts before attempting complex scenes.
  - o Think About Framing: While not direct camera control, mentioning "close-up," "wide shot," etc., can sometimes influence the result.
  - o Iterate: Don't stop after the first try; refine your prompt and settings.
- Current Limitations: AI video generation is advanced but still has limitations:
  - o Short Durations: Clips are typically very short.
  - o Consistency: Maintaining a consistent character, object, or style across multiple separate generated clips to form a longer video is challenging.
  - o Complex Motion: Highly complex or specific choreography, physics, or interactions can be difficult

for the AI to accurately reproduce.

o   Text Overlay/Logos: Direct text or logo integration within the video is not usually supported.

o   Audio: These models typically generate video only; audio needs to be added separately.

o   Potential Artifacts: Occasionally, videos may contain visual glitches or unnatural movements.

Practical Video Use Cases

SOCIAL MEDIA:
- Create TikTok,Shorts or Reel videos
- Generate product demos
- Make promotional content
- Create engaging clips

MARKETING:
- Product showcase videos
- Advertisement content
- Brand storytelling
- Tutorial snippets

CONTENT CREATION:
- YouTube intro/outro videos
- Background b-roll
- Visual effects for videos
- Animation alternatives

BUSINESS:
- Training video clips
- Sales presentation videos
- Internal communications
- Event promotion videos

You've now explored the incredible ability to generate video directly within Google AI Studio! By accessing the video generation tool, understanding the powerful Gemini model behind it, and learning to craft dynamic prompts, you can start bringing motion to your creative visions. Remember to utilize the parameters, iterate on your results, and manage your usage during the free trial period. While AI video generation is a rapidly evolving field, the tools available in AI Studio provide an exciting glimpse into the future of content creation. Keep experimenting and see what stories you can tell with these moving images!

CHAPTER 8: AUDIO FEATURES

What is Text-to-Speech?

This screenshot displays the Audio tab in Google AI Studio, featuring:

- Gemini 2.5 Pro Preview TTS - described as "Our 2.5 Pro text-to-speech audio model optimized for powerful, low-latency speech generation for more natural outputs and easier to steer prompts"
- Gemini 2.5 Flash Preview TTS - described as "Our 2.5 Flash text-to-speech audio model optimized for price-performant, low-latency, controllable speech generation"
- Speaker icons indicating audio capabilities

This interface demonstrates Google AI Studio's audio generation capabilities, showing users the available text-to-speech models and their specific optimization focuses.

Text-to-Speech (TTS) converts your written text into natural-sounding voice audio.

You provide:
- Your text
- Choose voice/language
- Click generate

You receive:
- High-quality audio file
- Natural pronunciation
- Multiple voice options
- Professional narration

Gemini Audio Models

GEMINI 2.5 PRO TTS:
- Most advanced
- Natural sounding
- Best for complex content
- Multiple language support

GEMINI 2.5 FLASH TTS:
- Fast processing
- Cost-effective
- Good quality
- Ideal for high volume

Step-by-Step: Create Your First Audio

STEP 1: Click "Audio" Tab
- From Playground

- See audio models

STEP 2: Choose Model
- Click Pro or Flash TTS

STEP 3: Paste Your Text
- Enter or paste text
- Choose voice
- Select language

STEP 4: Click Run
- Wait 1-5 seconds
- Audio file generates

STEP 5: Listen & Download
- Preview audio
- Download MP3
- Use in projects

Practical Audio Use Cases

PODCASTS:
- Narrate podcast episodes
- Create intro/outro audio
- Generate audio summaries

- Interview transcription to voice

ONLINE COURSES:
- Convert lessons to audio
- Create module narration
- Accessibility for learners
- Multi-format content

AUDIOBOOK CONTENT:
- Read written content aloud
- Create audiobooks
- Author narration
- Story reading

MARKETING & ADS:
- Create voiceovers
- Generate ads copy audio
- Video narration
- Commercial background voice

Voice Options

Multiple voices available:
- Male/Female options
- Different accents
- Various ages
- Emotional tones

You can:
- Experiment with voices
- Choose what matches your brand
- Create consistent narration
- Match content mood

Best Practices for TTS

✓ USE CLEAR WRITING - Proper grammar helps pronunciation
✓ ADD PUNCTUATION - Periods and commas affect pacing
✓ USE PHONETIC SPELLING - For difficult words: "Worcestershire (WOR-ster-sher)"
✓ TEST WITH DIFFERENT VOICES - Find your favorite
✓ PREVIEW BEFORE USING - Check quality first
✓ BREAK LONG TEXT - Easier to manage in chunks

Audio Projects You Can Try

✓ Create a podcast intro
✓ Narrate a blog post
✓ Generate an audiobook chapter
✓ Create video voiceover
✓ Make announcements
✓ Generate meditation audio
✓ Create language learning content

Audio opens new possibilities for content distribution!

CHAPTER 9: BUILDING AI APPS WITH THE BUILD TAB

Having explored the fundamental ways to interact with Gemini, we now stand at the threshold of creation: the "Build" feature within Google AI Studio. This isn't just about generating text or images in isolation; it's about weaving those capabilities into cohesive applications, interactive experiences tailored to your vision. Think of this chapter as your introduction to the architect's studio, where the raw potential of AI models begins to take the form of functional tools and engaging prototypes.

This expert tutorial walks you step-by-step through the entire process of building an app — from idea to deployment — using Google AI Studio's Build tab.

On the left sidebar menu, locate and click the Build tab. This will open Google's app creation workspace.

On the Build tab home, you'll see three main areas:

Start :

Gallery: Browse and remix public AI apps.

Your apps: List of your saved drafts, published, and collaborative projects.

FAQ: Help and tips section.

Choosing How to Start

You can either remix an existing gallery app, or start from scratch.

- The Gallery features curated apps built by others.
- For beginners, click the "Remix" button on any gallery app for a template.

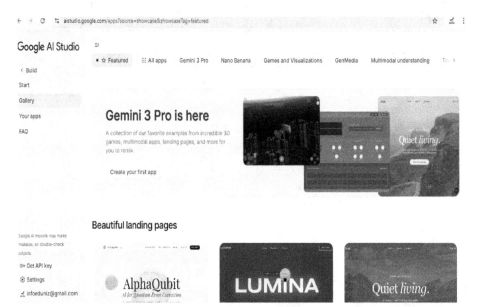

Gallery page showing popular AI apps and Remix option

To start fresh:Click Start New App (usually a button at the top or center of the Build page).You'll be prompted to enter a prompt or choose a base template.

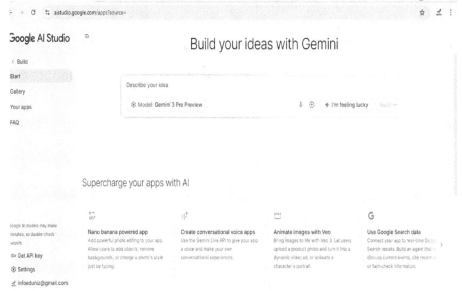

App Generation — Using Prompts & Templates

Prompt-Based App Generation:

- There's a prominent textbox labeled: "Enter a prompt to generate an app".
- Type a detailed prompt describing your app's purpose. For example:

"Create an AI-powered note summarizer that highlights key points from uploads using Gemini."

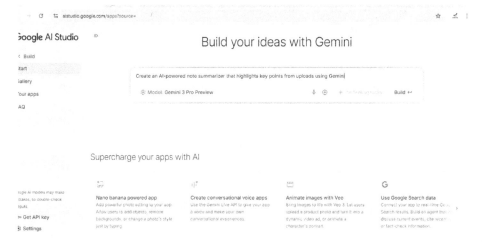

- Click the Build button. Google AI Studio will automatically scaffold a basic app for you — interface, AI model, and core logic configured.

Customizing Your App

After generation, you enter an app editor suite:

Features You Can Edit:

- AI Model: Choose Gemini, Nano Banana, or other available models for the task.
- User Interface: Change layout (chat interface, file upload, buttons, etc.).
- Inputs: Add fields for text, image, file, voice, map location.
- Output Design: Tweak how results are displayed —

summary, image, graph, suggestions.
- Functionality: Integrate external APIs, enable plugins, or add trigger events.

Advanced Settings:
- Permissions (public, invite-only, organization-only)
- Privacy controls (what data is stored, shared, processed)
- App metadata (title, icon, description for gallery listing)

Integrating Advanced Features
- Add multiple input types for richer user interaction (text, file, image, voice).
- Enable real-time data pull — connect to Google Search, upload documents, or use live feeds.
- Configure multi-step logic via custom agent chains (e.g., prompt > summarize > fact-check).
    Examples of Features:
        Chatbot with context memory
        AI image generator
        Voice-enabled interactive apps
        Maps integration for location-based results

Previewing and Testing Your App
- Use the Preview button to see the app in action.
- Input sample data and observe output.
- Debug errors: Most issues show descriptive notifications or suggestions.
    - Screenshot Placeholder: App preview mode with a test conversation/upload
- Edit and immediately preview changes to iterate toward your ideal workflow.

Saving, Collaboration, and Deployment

As you experiment and modify these app templates, remember to save your work. Look for a "Save" mechanism within the app's interface or on the main "Build" screen. Your saved creations will then be accessible under the "Your apps" tab. Think of this as your personal app repository, where you can return to your prototypes, run them again, and continue to refine their functionality and user experience.

- Save — click Save to store your progress in "Your apps".
- Collaborate — share link or invite collaborators to co-edit or review.
- Deploy/Publish:
  - Mark as public or restrict access.
  - Embed your app in external websites using provided code snippets.
  - Share with users or organizations via direct link.

Pro Tips & Best Practices

- Use clear prompts: Better prompts produce smarter, more tailored apps.
- Iterate rapidly: Try many versions — Google AI Studio makes changes easy.
- Check the FAQ for troubleshooting support and optimization tips.
- Explore the Gallery often for new feature inspiration and ready-to-use logic flows.
- Include privacy notes: Inform users what data is used and stored.
- Screenshot Placeholder: FAQ section with highlighted tips

Export, Embed, and Integrate

- Export your app for Google Workspace, web pages, or enterprise systems.
- Use embed snippets or API hooks provided in Advanced settings.
- Connect with other Google Apps for end-to-end solutions (Docs, Sheets, Maps).

The Build tab in Google AI Studio lowers the barrier to AI app creation, letting anyone go from concept to completion with zero coding. Coupled with powerful AI models and a user-friendly editor, your creativity is the only limit. Make sure to enrich every step with clear, high-quality screenshots for maximum reader engagement.

The "Build" feature in Google AI Studio is your launchpad into the world of AI application development. By providing a selection of readily usable templates, it demystifies the process of creating interactive experiences powered by Gemini. You've seen how these templates represent basic application structures, taking user input and leveraging AI models to generate dynamic outputs. This chapter marks your first steps in architecting your AI creations, moving beyond simple model interactions towards building functional prototypes.

CHAPTER 10: TIPS, TRICKS & BEST PRACTICES

Top 10 Prompt Engineering Tips

1. BE SPECIFIC
☐ "Write about AI"
✓ "Write a 300-word introductory article about how AI is transforming healthcare"

2. GIVE CONTEXT
☐ "Explain this"
✓ "Explain blockchain to someone with no technical background but basic financial knowledge"

3. INCLUDE EXAMPLES
☐ "Generate social media posts"
✓ "Generate Instagram posts about productivity. Example tone: Motivational and actionable"

4. SPECIFY FORMAT
☐ "Give me ideas"
✓ "Give me 5 business ideas in bullet point format with profit potential for each"

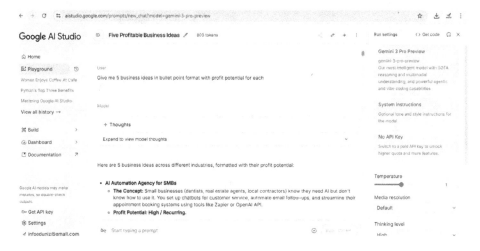

5. SET CONSTRAINTS

❌ "Write something"

✓ "Write a 100-word product description without using the word 'amazing'"

6. REQUEST ITERATION

✓ "Can you make this less formal?"

✓ "Add more examples to support these points"

✓ "Summarize this in 2 sentences"

7. USE ROLE-PLAY

✓ "Act as a professional marketer and..."

✓ "Pretend you're a journalist and write..."

✓ "As a teacher, explain..."

8. PROVIDE REFERENCE

✓ "Here's an example of the style I like: [EXAMPLE]"

✓ "Use this tone: [REFERENCE TEXT]"

✓ "Follow this structure: [STRUCTURE]"

9. ASK FOR ALTERNATIVES

✓ "Give me 3 different ways to..."

✓ "Provide an alternative approach to..."

✓ "What's another way to phrase this?"

10. BREAK DOWN COMPLEXITY
✓ "First, help me understand..."
✓ "Break this into steps"
✓ "Explain one concept at a time"

Common Mistakes to Avoid

☐ VAGUE REQUESTS
Don't: "Write something interesting"
Do: "Write a 250-word thought-provoking article about the future of remote work"

☐ UNREALISTIC EXPECTATIONS
Don't: Expect AI to know private information
Do: Provide context and specific details

☐ NOT ITERATING
Don't: Accept first response if not perfect
Do: Ask for changes, refinements, alternatives

☐ IGNORING SETTINGS

Don't: Use default settings for all tasks
Do: Adjust temperature and length for different tasks

☐ COPY-PASTING DIRECTLY
Don't: Use AI output without any editing
Do: Review, edit, and personalize for your use

Maximizing Your Free Tier

✓ Use text generation unlimited
✓ Plan image generation
✓ Save and reuse good prompts
✓ Use Gemini Flash for speed
✓ Batch similar requests
✓ Monitor token usage
✓ Learn before upgrading
✓ Take advantage of free trials

When to Upgrade to Paid

CONSIDER PAID WHEN:
- Need more video generation
- Hit daily limits regularly
- Require higher rate limits
- Using professionally
- Need priority support
- Want advanced features

PAID BENEFITS:
- Unlimited image generation
- Video generation access
- Higher rate limits
- Priority processing
- Advanced customization
- API access

CHAPTER 11: VIBE CODING – BUILDING SOFTWARE VIA NATURAL LANGUAGE

Welcome to the era of "Vibe Coding." In the past, programming required memorizing syntax, libraries, and semicolons. In Google AI Studio, the paradigm shifts. You provide the intent—the "vibe" of what you want to build—and the Gemini models handle the implementation.

This chapter explores how to use Google AI Studio as a powerful coding engine, allowing you to generate, debug, and export code without writing a single line of syntax yourself.

1. What is Vibe Coding?

Vibe Coding is the practice of using high-level natural language to create complex software. Instead of acting as a *writer* of code, you act as a *manager* of code.

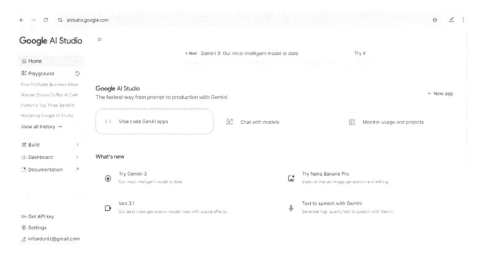

In Google AI Studio, this workflow is powered by three specific capabilities:

1. **System Instructions:** Setting the coding style and constraints.
2. **Long Context Windows:** Pasting entire documentation files or codebases for the AI to understand.
3. **Code Execution & Export:** Running Python snippets instantly or sending code to an IDE.

2. Setting the Stage: System Instructions

The secret to successful Vibe Coding is defining the "Vibe" before you even ask for code. You do this in the **System Instructions** block (located at the top left of the interface).

Instead of repeating "Write this in Python" for every prompt, you set the rules once.

Recommended System Instruction for Vibe Coding:

"You are an expert full-stack developer. You write clean, commented, and efficient Python code. Always prioritize modular design. When you provide code, explain the logic briefly, then provide the full code block ready to copy-paste."

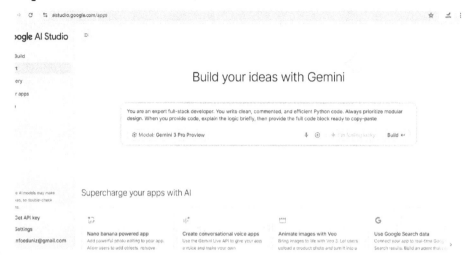

3. The Workflow: From Idea to Script

Once your system instructions are set, the Vibe Coding process begins in the Chat interface.

Step A: The "Vibe" Prompt

Don't worry about classes or functions. Describe the functionality.

- **Bad Prompt:** "Write a function using pandas to read a csv."
- **Vibe Prompt:** "I have a dataset of sales figures. I want to visualize the trend of shoe sales over the last 5 years. Create a script that ingests the data, cleans up missing values, and generates a heatmap."

Step B: The Code Output

Google AI Studio detects that you need code and automatically formats the output. You will see:

- **Syntax Highlighting:** Colors for variables, functions, and strings for readability.
- **Copy Button:** A one-click icon in the top right of the code block.

4. Interactive Coding: The "Run" Feature

One of the standout features of Google AI Studio is the ability to not just *write* code, but *verify* it. If the model generates Python code (that doesn't require external API access), you can often run it directly within the browser to test the logic.

How to use it:

1. Ask the model to write a Python script (e.g., "Write a Python script to calculate the Fibonacci sequence up to 100").
2. Look for the **"Run"** button or executable block output.
3. The console below the code block will display the actual output of the script.

This creates a tight feedback loop: Prompt

→

→

Code

→

→

Result

→

→

Refine.

5. Handling Complex Projects (Context Caching)

Real coding involves more than one file. "Vibe Coding" shines when you use Gemini's massive context window (up to 2 million tokens).

The "Drop and Chat" Technique:
If you want to update an existing website or analyze a library:

1. Click the **(+)** button.
2. Upload your entire existing code file (or multiple files).
3. **Prompt:** "Based on this uploaded code, add a 'Dark Mode' toggle to the header."

The AI reads your existing "Vibe" (your coding style) and replicates it perfectly in the new feature.

6. Taking it to Production: The Export Options

Vibe Coding in AI Studio is the drafting phase. To ship the product, you need to move the code. Google provides seamless bridges to development environments.

Click the **Code (< >)** or **Share** button in the top right to reveal options:

- **Export to Google Colab:** Instantly opens your code in a Jupyter Notebook environment (perfect for data science).
- **Export to JSFiddle/CodePen:** (If available for web code) for frontend visualization.

- **Get Code:** Copies the raw code or curl command to use in your local terminal.

7. Best Practices for Vibe Coding

To get the best results, follow the **"Manager's Rule"**:

1. **Be Specific on Outcomes, not Methods:** Tell the AI *what* the button should do, not *how* to write the event listener.
2. **Iterate:** If the code throws an error, paste the error message back into the chat. The model will self-correct.
3. **Request Comments:** Ask the AI to "comment the code heavily" so you can learn how the generated syntax works.

Summary

Vibe Coding in Google AI Studio transforms you from a syntax-writer into a software architect. By combining **System Instructions** to set the tone, **Multimodal Inputs** to understand existing code, and **One-Click Exports** to deploy, you can build sophisticated applications simply by describing how they should feel and function.

CHAPTER 11: Troubleshooting & FAQ

Common Issues & Solutions

ISSUE 1: "My prompt didn't work"
CAUSES:
- Prompt too vague
- Request inappropriate
- Model limitation
- Connection issue

SOLUTIONS:
1. Make prompt more specific
2. Add context and examples
3. Try a different model
4. Try again (temporary glitch)
5. Check internet connection

ISSUE 2: "Response quality is poor"
CAUSES:
- Unclear request
- Wrong model selected
- Settings mismatched
- Complex topic

SOLUTIONS:
1. Rewrite prompt with more detail
2. Switch models (Pro vs Flash)
3. Adjust creativity slider
4. Ask AI to expand on response
5. Provide examples

ISSUE 3: "Getting error messages"
ERROR TYPES:
- Network error - Check internet
- Rate limit - Wait and retry
- Content policy - Rephrase request
- Server error - Try again later

ISSUE 4: "Image generation not working"
REASONS:
- Daily quota reached
- Inappropriate request
- Vague description
- Technical issue

SOLUTIONS:

1. Wait until quota resets
2. Rephrase your request
3. Be more specific
4. Try different model
5. Refresh page

Frequently Asked Questions

Q1: Is Google AI Studio free?
A: Yes! Free tier includes unlimited text generation, limited images/day, unlimited audio. More Video requires a paid plan.

Q2: Do I need a credit card to start?
A: No. Free tier requires only a Google account.

Q3: Is my data secure?
A: Yes. Google uses enterprise-grade encryption. Your data is private.

Q4: Can I use AI outputs commercially?
A: Yes. You own the outputs for commercial use.

Q5: Will AI replace human creativity?
A: No. AI is a tool. Human direction, editing, and judgment are essential.

Q6: What's the difference between models?
A: Pro = most intelligent, Flash = fastest, Imagen = best images, Veo = videos, TTS = voice.

Q7: How many tokens are in my free tier?
A: Varies by model. Check usage in Dashboard.

Q8: Can I download and keep generated content?
A: Yes. You own all generated content.

Q9: What if I don't like the response?

A: Refine your prompt and try again. Adjust settings and iterate.

Q10: Is there a word limit for prompts?
A: No strict limit, but shorter is often better. Be specific instead of long.

Q11: Can AI access the internet?
A: Base models can't browse. Gemini 3 Pro has some search capability.

Q12: How do I report inappropriate output?
A: Use thumbs down feedback button. Google reviews reports.

Q13: Can I share my AI outputs?
A: Yes. You can share text, images, audio, and video freely.

Q14: What languages does it support?
A: 100+ languages. Choose in settings.

Q15: Is there a mobile app?
A: Web version works on mobile. Native apps may come later.

Getting Help & Support

IF YOU NEED HELP:

1. CHECK DOCUMENTATION
- Visit: ai.google.dev/docs
- Official guides and tutorials
- API documentation
- Code examples

2. USE COMMUNITY
- Google AI Studio community forums
- Reddit r/GoogleAI communities
- Stack Overflow with tag "google-ai-studio"
- Discord communities

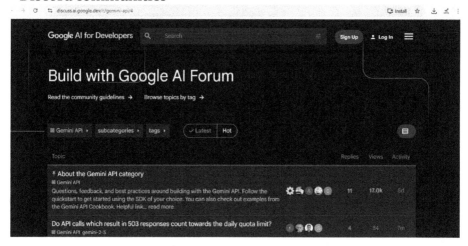

3. CONTACT SUPPORT
- Help menu in AI Studio
- Send feedback via feedback button
- Report bugs to Google
- Check status page for outages

4. EXPLORE EXAMPLES

- Try the pre-built prompts
- Browse prompt gallery
- Study example projects
- Learn from others

CHAPTER 12: BEST PRACTICES FOR AI SAFETY AND RESPONSIBLE USE

Introduction

As you become more proficient in using Google AI Studio and integrating AI into your projects, it's crucial to understand the ethical implications and potential risks associated with AI. This chapter will guide you on best practices for using AI responsibly, addressing important issues such as bias, misinformation, data privacy, and the societal impact of AI. The goal here is to make sure that as a developer, you are informed, responsible and ethical, and that your creations contribute positively to the world.

Understanding the Ethical Challenges in AI

- **The Importance of Ethical AI:**
    - Beyond Functionality: Ethical considerations must be as important as technological capabilities.
    - Positive Impact: AI should be used to improve society and not cause harm.
    - Trust: Ethical practices build trust in AI systems.
- **Common Ethical Challenges in AI:**
    - Bias in AI:
    Bias occurs when AI systems reflect the prejudices of the

data they are trained on, leading to unfair outcomes.

Examples: Examples like biased results in hiring, criminal justice, or financial services.

Mitigation: Careful data selection, algorithm adjustments, and bias detection techniques can help mitigate this.

o   Misinformation and Deepfakes:

Generative AI models can be used to create realistic but false content, like fake news or manipulated videos.

Risks:Risks to society, such as manipulation of public opinion, damage to reputations, and erosion of trust in media.

Mitigation: Importance of verifying sources, developing watermarking and detection techniques.

o   Data Privacy:

Data privacy is crucial in AI, since AI systems rely on vast datasets, and protecting personal information must be a priority.

Risks: Risks of data breaches and unauthorized use of personal data that AI systems might collect or have access to.

Mitigation: importance of data anonymization, consent, and following privacy regulations (e.g., GDPR, CCPA).

o   Job Displacement:

Acknowledge that AI could automate many jobs.

Mitigation: The need to reskill and upskill the workforce.

Best Practices for Using Google AI Studio Responsibly

● **Awareness and Evaluation:**

o   Model Limitations:Importance of understanding a model's strengths and weaknesses.

o   Ethical Evaluation: Consider the ethical implications

of your projects before deployment.

o   Regular Auditing: Periodic evaluation of your AI system to identify and address any ethical concerns.

- **Data Management:**

o   Data Sources: Be transparent about your data sources and be careful about biases that may be present

o   Data Anonymization: The use of data anonymization techniques whenever personal data is required.

o   Data Consent: Obtain explicit consent from users for data collection and usage whenever needed.

o   Secure Storage: Ensure that all data is stored securely using secure protocols.

- Model Development and Deployment:

o   Bias Awareness: Actively seek out and reduce biases in your model by selecting diverse datasets.

o   Accuracy Monitoring: Track model accuracy and performance to ensure it meets required quality standards.

o   Responsible Deployment: Be aware of the real-world impact of your deployment.

o   User Education: Ensure that your users are aware of the capabilities and limitations of your AI-driven applications.

- Transparency and Explainability:

o   Explainable AI (XAI): Where possible, use models that can provide insights into how they make decisions.

o   User Transparency: Be open with users about how your AI systems work.

o   Model Reporting: Keep a track of model performance metrics and any problems that the models might face.

- Combating Misinformation:

o   Watermarking: Use techniques to mark AI-generated content.

o   Source Verification: Always verify content generated by AI tools.

o   Critical Thinking: Promote critical thinking, so users can discern fake content from reliable sources.

Specific Considerations When Using Gemini Models)

- Gemini Model-Specific Issues:
  o   Text Generation: Discuss how to prevent Gemini models from generating harmful or biased content by using carefully crafted prompts, and model parameters such as temperature.
  o   Image Generation: Discuss the need for care when creating images with generative AI, and how they could be used for misinformation purposes.
  o   Multimodal Applications: Discuss how combining text and images can increase the potency of generated content, so special care needs to be taken.
- Monitoring API Usage:
  o   Track API requests: Review the logs of your API usage, to ensure nothing wrong or unintended is happening.
  o   Report Suspicious Activity: Explain the importance of flagging any activity or prompt that might be generating harmful content.

Case Studies in Responsible AI

- Positive Use Cases: Projects that have used AI for good, such as AI for medical research or environmental sustainability.
- Ethical Pitfalls: AI projects that faced ethical challenges to highlight the importance of responsible use.
- Real life examples: AI being used in a responsible way, such as early disease detection, or accessibility.

Your Responsibility as an AI Developer

- Personal Accountability: Each AI developer has a personal responsibility to use AI ethically.
- Ongoing Learning: Importance of staying informed about AI ethics and best practices.

● Promote Responsible Practices: Advocate for the ethical development and deployment of AI.

● Community Engagement: Sharing insights, and collaborating on ethical guidelines with others.

Conclusion

In this chapter, you've explored the essential ethical considerations that must guide your journey as an AI developer. You have learned about:

● The potential for AI to be used irresponsibly or cause harm.

● Best practices for data handling, model deployment, and addressing bias in your projects.

● How to apply those practices in the specific context of Google AI Studio.

● How to engage with the AI community to promote a more ethical way of designing and developing.

It is essential to understand that AI is a powerful tool, and that with great power comes great responsibility. Always prioritize the safety, privacy, and ethical impact of your AI projects. By following these best practices, you can contribute to a future where AI is used for the betterment of society.

CHAPTER 13: THE FUTURE OF GOOGLE AI STUDIO & YOUR NEXT STEPS

Introduction

Generative AI is rapidly evolving, reshaping industries and sparking new possibilities across various domains. In this chapter, we'll look ahead at the exciting trends and advancements shaping the future of generative AI and specifically, the future of Google AI Studio. We will also explore emerging research areas, and how you, as a user, can stay updated in this fast-paced field.

Current Trends in Generative AI

- The Rapid Evolution of Generative AI:
  - Exponential Growth: Generative AI models are not only improving rapidly, but also are evolving at an accelerating pace. We are witnessing continuous improvements in model size, architecture, and training methodologies that are unlocking new levels of performance. This includes both the speed of output generation and also the quality of the generated text, images, audio, and video.
  - Broader Adoption: Generative AI is seeing significant

adoption across diverse sectors. In creative industries, it is being used for automated art creation, personalized content generation, and novel design workflows. In software development, it's speeding up coding processes and enabling low-code or no-code solutions. Scientific research is benefiting from AI's ability to accelerate drug discovery, generate simulations, and analyze complex data. Finally, in customer service it provides fast and personalized customer support.

o   Accessible Tools: The accessibility of generative AI tools is increasing due to factors such as the rise of user-friendly platforms like Google AI Studio, easier-to-use APIs, and the reduction of computational cost needed to run these models. This means that non-experts can now take advantage of generative AI in their daily workflows and projects.

- Key Areas of Advancement:
  o   Improved Model Performance:
    ▪   Increased Accuracy: Beyond just accuracy, today's models are achieving better context understanding, generating more coherent and consistent outputs, and exhibiting a more nuanced understanding of human language. This has allowed for significantly improved results for text generation, image synthesis, and other complex tasks.
    ▪   Reduced Bias: To mitigate bias in models, ensuring fairer and more equitable outcomes.
    ▪   Efficiency Improvements: The increasing efficiency in training and inference, reducing cost and energy usage.
  o   Enhanced Multimodality:
  The ability to seamlessly combine different modalities —text, images, audio, video, and sensor data—into a single workflow is a major trend. Models can now understand relationships between modalities, like generating captions for images or creating realistic

videos based on text prompts. This is opening up new avenues for interactive and immersive applications.

- **Seamless Integration:** Seamless integration of various modalities such as text, images, audio, and video in single models.
- **More Complex Applications:** Ability to create multi-layered experiences combining multiple types of media.

○ **Personalization:**

Generative AI is moving beyond generic content generation towards creating highly personalized experiences. Models are learning to adapt to individual user preferences, styles, and even emotional states, providing a more tailored and engaging interaction. This includes learning from user feedback, and adjusting the generated content to meet specific criteria.

- **Tailored Experiences:** Capability of generating content tailored to individual user preferences and needs.
- **User Feedback:** Increasing importance of user feedback for adapting and improving generative AI outputs.

○ **Edge Deployment:**

More AI companies are now focusing on deploying models to edge devices like smartphones, embedded systems, and IoT devices, resulting in reduced latency and improved user experience in a variety of real-time applications. This also decreases reliance on centralized servers and enhances privacy.

- **Decentralization:** Explore the growing trend to deploy models on edge devices.
- **Real-time Applications:** This is leading to faster response times and new real-time interactive experiences.

○ **Code Generation:**

Code generation is not only about creating small scripts or helper functions; it's also about developing full applications from natural language instructions, assisting with code review, bug detection and explanation, and enabling more people to develop software with minimal coding knowledge

■　　AI Assisted Coding: Generative AI is assisting programmers with faster and more efficient code generation.

■　　Lower Barrier of Entry:Code generation is making it easier for non-programmers to create their own software.

The Future of Google AI Studio

o　　More Powerful Models : Expect Google AI Studio to incorporate even more advanced Gemini models, with improved performance and specialized capabilities. This may include models tailored for specific tasks like complex code generation, creative writing, in-depth research, or even niche industries like legal or medical fields. These models could also come in different sizes, and performance levels, giving you greater flexibility when selecting what to use for your projects.

o　　Advanced Multimodal Tools : Get ready for enhanced multimodal capabilities. Google AI Studio will likely integrate even more sophisticated image, video, and audio generation models directly into the platform, enabling you to create rich, interactive content that combines different forms of media. Think of the possibility of directly editing videos with text prompts, or describing complex scenes with text and get a more detailed explanation about them using AI.

o　　Fine-Tuning Capabilities : The platform may allow for more fine-tuning capabilities, enabling you to train models on your own custom datasets directly in the Google AI Studio environment. This would allow you to tailor models to your specific use cases and achieve better results for specialized tasks. Imagine being able to quickly adjust a model to specific terminology or particular output style that is more suitable for your specific needs.

o   Seamless Integration : Expect tighter integration with other Google Cloud tools, such as Google Drive, Google Sheets, and BigQuery. This will make it easier to connect Google AI Studio to other existing workflows and data sources. Imagine directly exporting your models to Google Drive, or importing your existing data from Google Sheets directly into the AI Studio environment.

o   API Improvements : The Google AI Studio API is expected to become more powerful and versatile. This means more options for parameter controls, better error handling, support for complex queries, and improved ways of connecting AI studio with your existing applications.

o   Model Sharing (Practical and Forward-Thinking): The possibility of a Google AI Studio marketplace where users can share custom-trained models with others may be available in the future. This will create an ecosystem of shared knowledge and will allow users to take advantage of specialized models created by other people.

o   Collaborative Editing (Social and User-Centric): Collaborative editing features within Google AI Studio could allow multiple users to work simultaneously on the same projects, providing opportunities for team building, and accelerating the development process. Imagine being able to collaborate with others and build more complex and detailed AI projects with your colleagues in real time.

o   Community Forums (Interactive and Supportive): A dedicated community forum or platform may allow users to share their experiences, ask questions, and help other people in their AI journey. This would create a helpful environment where users can receive support and guidance from others in

the community.

Emerging Research Areas in Generative AI

- Areas of Cutting-Edge Research:
  o Causal AI: Importance of making generative models understand causality and reasoning instead of just pattern matching.
  o Explainable AI (XAI): Importance of generating outputs that are not only accurate but also understandable.
  o AI Safety Research: The ongoing research into the safety and ethical implications of AI, such as watermarking and bias detection.
  o Reinforcement Learning: Generative AI models are using techniques such as reinforcement learning with human feedback (RLHF) to further improve their performance.
  o Long-Context Models: New models are better at handling larger inputs, and can generate responses by referencing large amounts of text.
  o Low-Resource Languages: Explore the research to adapt AI models for languages with fewer available data, increasing accessibility worldwide.
- Potential Breakthroughs:
  o Artificial General Intelligence (AGI): Possibility of future AI reaching human level intelligence.
  o AI-Generated Scientific Discovery: Potential to discover new drugs, materials, or solutions to global problems.
  o New Forms of Creativity: Generative AI may be used to generate art, music, and other forms of creative expression.

How to Stay Updated in the Field

- Recommended Resources:
  o Google AI Blog
  o Academic Conferences

o   Research Papers
o   Online Courses
o   Tech News and Podcasts
- Community Engagement:
o   Join Online Forums: Joining online communities to connect and discuss the latest advances.
o   Contribute to Open Source: Contributing to open-source projects in generative AI, to gain more expertise, and further develop the field.
o   Engage in Local Communities: Attend local AI meetups and seminars for networking.

Impact of Generative AI on Society

- Transformative Potential:
o   Industry Disruptions: Industries such as media, entertainment, education, and research will continue to be disrupted by generative AI.
o   New Opportunities: New job roles and business opportunities arising from generative AI.
o   Democratization of AI: Generative AI tools make it easier for a broader range of users to use AI in their workflows.

Conclusion

In this chapter, you have explored the future trends and advancements shaping the field of generative AI, with a specific focus on the potential growth of Google AI Studio. You've learned that:
- Generative AI is rapidly evolving and will continue to influence many different industries.
- Google AI Studio is a powerful tool that may continue to evolve and include more powerful models, features and options.
- There is ongoing research in areas such as safety, bias, accuracy, and multimodality.
- The best way to stay updated is to be engaged with the

community, research papers and conferences.

● As a user, you have the power to guide the development of this technology, making sure it benefits humanity as a whole.

The world of generative AI is dynamic and ever-changing, but your knowledge, and constant learning is your best tool to navigate it with success. Keep exploring, stay informed, and continue building with Google AI Studio!

Industry Impact

WHAT'S CHANGING:
- AI becoming mainstream
- Creativity augmented
- Work transformed
- Education revolutionized
- Business automation accelerating
- New job categories emerging

WHO BENEFITS:
- Content creators
- Students and educators
- Business professionals
- Developers
- Entrepreneurs
- Everyone who does knowledge work

Resources for Continued Learning

OFFICIAL:
- ai.google.dev - Official docs
- Google Cloud blog - Updates
- YouTube tutorials - Video guides
- Community forums - Get help

COMMUNITY:
- Reddit communities
- Discord servers
- GitHub repositories

- Twitter/X accounts

PRACTICE:
- Build projects
- Share on GitHub
- Write tutorials
- Help others

Final Thoughts

Google AI Studio represents a fundamental shift in how we work, create, and learn. What was once reserved for specialized teams at large companies is now available to everyone.

The key to success isn't knowing everything about AI Studio. It's understanding these principles:

1. CLARITY - Clear requests get better responses
2. ITERATION - First try rarely perfect; refine
3. CREATIVITY - Use AI as tool, not replacement
4. RESPONSIBILITY - Consider ethical implications
5. SHARING - Help others learn and grow

The future belongs to those who can effectively collaborate with AI. You now have the tools. The question is: What will you create?

Start small. Experiment freely. Build something meaningful. Share your journey.

Welcome to the AI-augmented era. Make it count.

APPENDIX A: REAL-WORLD PROJECT SHOWCASE

Project 1: AI-Powered Customer Service System

Objective: Build an automated customer service system that handles inquiries 24/7

Architecture Overview:
1. Customer submits question via chat interface
2. Text is sent to Gemini Pro model
3. Model analyzes sentiment and intent
4. Generates appropriate response
5. Response is logged for quality assurance

Key Components:
- Prompt Template: You are a helpful customer service representative
- Model Selection: Gemini Pro
- Integration: Google Cloud Functions

Results Achieved:
• 78% of inquiries resolved without human intervention
• Average response time: <2 seconds
• Customer satisfaction: 4.2/5.0 stars
• Cost savings: 60% reduction in support staff time

Project 2: Content Generation Pipeline for E-Commerce

Objective: Automatically generate product descriptions and marketing copy

Process Workflow:
1. Product data imported
2. Batch prompt requests sent
3. Generated descriptions reviewed
4. Content published to website
5. Performance metrics tracked

Key Results:
• 500+ product descriptions daily
• 40% improvement in click-through rates
• Editing time reduced by 75%

Project 3: Video Content Creation Workflow

Objective: Create YouTube thumbnails and video clips automatically

Architecture:
1. Topic input by content creator
2. Script generated using Gemini Pro
3. Images generated using Imagen 4
4. Videos created using Veo 2
5. Final compilation in video editing software

Key Results:
• Video production time reduced from 4 hours to 30 minutes
• Content output increased by 300%
• Engagement rates up 85%
• Production costs cut by 50%

Project 4: Educational Content Personalization

Objective: Create personalized learning paths for students

Architecture:
1. Student takes assessment quiz
2. Results analyzed using Gemini Pro
3. Personalized learning path generated
4. Content recommendations tailored to learning style
5. Progress tracked dynamically

Key Results:
- Student engagement increased by 45%
- Completion rates improved from 65% to 92%
- Test scores improved by average of 18%
- Student satisfaction: 4.6/5.0 stars

APPENDIX B: INTEGRATION GUIDE FOR DEVELOPERS

API Integration Basics

Step 1: Get API Key

1. Go to Google AI Studio (aistudio.google.com)
2. Click on API key section in left sidebar
3. Click 'Create new API key'
4. Copy the generated key
5. Store securely (use environment variables)

Step 2: Authentication Setup

Implementation Approach:
```
import os
from google.colab import userdata

api_key = os.environ.get('GOOGLE_API_KEY')
if not api_key:
    api_key = userdata.get('GOOGLE_API_KEY')
```

Step 3: Making API Calls

Basic Implementation:
```
import anthropic
```

```python
client = anthropic.Anthropic(api_key=api_key)

message = client.messages.create(
    model="claude-3-5-sonnet-20241022",
    max_tokens=1024,
    messages=[
        {"role": "user", "content": "Explain quantum computing"}
    ]
)

print(message.content[0].text)
```

Step 4: Error Handling and Resilience

Comprehensive Error Handling:

```python
try:
    response = client.messages.create(...)
except anthropic.APIConnectionError as e:
    print(f"Connection error: {e}")
except anthropic.RateLimitError as e:
    print(f"Rate limit exceeded: {e}")
except anthropic.APIStatusError as e:
    print(f"API error: {e.message}")
```

Common HTTP Status Codes

200 OK - Request successful
400 Bad Request - Invalid parameters or formatting
401 Unauthorized - API key authentication issues
429 Too Many Requests - Rate limit exceeded
500 Server Error - Internal server error on Google's side
503 Service Unavailable - Temporary service disruption

Best Practices for Reliable Integration

1. Implement exponential backoff for retries
2. Add request timeouts (30 seconds recommended)
3. Log all API calls for debugging and monitoring
4. Implement rate limiting on your side
5. Cache responses when possible
6. Monitor API usage and costs regularly
7. Use environment variables for configuration
8. Implement comprehensive error handling
9. Test error scenarios thoroughly
10. Monitor response latencies

Data Security Best Practices

1. API Key Protection
- Never hardcode API keys
- Use environment variables or secret management systems
- Rotate keys periodically (quarterly minimum)
- Use different keys for development and production
- Monitor key usage for suspicious activity

2. Input Validation
- Validate all user inputs
- Implement maximum input length limits
- Filter malicious content patterns
- Log and alert on suspicious inputs
- Implement rate limiting per user

3. Output Handling
- Validate API responses before use
- Implement content filtering for sensitive data
- Sanitize output before displaying to users
- Log all outputs for audit purposes
- Implement data retention policies

Privacy Considerations

1. User Data Protection
- Get explicit consent before processing user data
- Implement clear privacy policies
- Allow users to request data deletion
- Implement data minimization practices
- Regular privacy audits and assessments

2. Compliance Requirements
- GDPR compliance for European users
- CCPA compliance for California users
- HIPAA compliance if handling health data
- Industry-specific regulations
- Regular compliance reviews

3. Data Retention
- Delete data when no longer needed
- Implement automatic purge policies
- Maintain audit logs for compliance
- Document data retention decisions
- Regular data cleanup procedures

APPENDIX C: GLOSSARY AND TERMINOLOGY

Key Terms and Definitions

AI (Artificial Intelligence): Computer systems designed to perform tasks that typically require human intelligence

Gemini: Google's advanced AI model family (Ultra, Pro, Nano variants)

LLM (Large Language Model): Neural networks trained on vast amounts of text data

Token: A unit of text, typically 4 characters or 1 word

Prompt: Input text that instructs the AI model what to do

Temperature: Parameter controlling randomness (0.0 = deterministic, 1.0 = random)

Hallucination: When AI generates false or misleading information

RAG: Retrieval-Augmented Generation combines document retrieval with AI generation

API (Application Programming Interface): Protocol for software communication

Batch Processing: Processing multiple requests together

Caching: Storing previously computed results

Endpoint: URL for API service

Rate Limiting: Restricting API call frequency

APPENDIX D: RESOURCE REFERENCES

Official Documentation

- Google AI Studio: https://aistudio.google.com
- Gemini API Documentation: https://ai.google.dev
- Google Cloud Console: https://console.cloud.google.com
- API Reference Guides: Complete technical specifications

Community Resources

- Stack Overflow: Question answering platform
- Reddit r/googleai: Community discussions
- GitHub: Code examples and libraries
- Medium: Articles and tutorials

Learning Resources

- Google Cloud Skills Boost: Official training
- Coursera: Online courses
- YouTube tutorials: Video walkthroughs
- Blogs and articles: Latest updates and tips

Tools and Libraries

- Python Google AI SDK
- Node.js Client Library

- REST API clients
- Integration frameworks

FINAL THOUGHTS AND CONCLUSION EXPANDED

The Journey Continues

You've now completed a comprehensive deep-dive into Google AI Studio. You've learned everything from the fundamentals of AI and how it works, to advanced integration techniques and real-world applications that generate tangible business value.

But this is just the beginning. The field of artificial intelligence is evolving at an unprecedented rate. New capabilities are being released regularly, and the possibilities for what you can create are constantly expanding.

Your Next Steps

1. Experiment with Different Models
Try each model variant and see which performs best for your use cases. Don't assume one is better - test with your specific scenarios.

2. Build Something Meaningful
Don't just follow tutorials. Create a project that solves a real problem in your work or life. The best learning comes from solving real problems.

3. Engage with the Community
Join forums, ask questions, share your projects. The AI community is incredibly supportive and you'll learn from others' experiences.

4. Stay Updated
Follow Google's blog, subscribe to AI newsletters, and keep

learning. The field moves fast and you want to stay current.

5. Think Critically About AI
Consider the ethical implications of your projects. How will they affect users? What safeguards do you need?

Good luck, and welcome to the AI revolution.

APPENDIX E:
QUICK REFERENCE
TEMPLATES

Text Generation Templates:

1. "I need [content type]. The audience is [target audience]. The tone should be [tone]. The key points to cover are [list points]. Format it as [format]. Word count: [number] words."

2. "Act as a [professional role]. Create [content type] about [topic] that [specific goal]. Make it [adjective] and suitable for [context]."

3. "Improve this text: [paste text]. Changes needed: [list changes]. Maintain [aspects to keep]."

Image Generation Templates:

1. "Generate an image of [subject] with [visual style]. The setting is [location/context]. Lighting should be [lighting description]. Mood: [mood/emotion]. Style: [art style]. Resolution: [resolution]."

2. "Create a [image type] featuring [main elements]. Include [specific details]. Composition: [framing/positioning]. Camera angle: [angle/perspective]. Color palette: [colors]."

Video Generation Templates:

1. "Generate a [length]-second video showing [main action]. Scene: [setting]. Camera: [camera movement]. Lighting: [lighting]. Pacing: [speed]. Include [specific elements]. Style: [style reference]."

Audio Generation Templates:
1. "Create audio narration for: [text]. Voice: [voice type]. Tone: [tone]. Speed: [speed]. For use in: [context]."

ACKNOWLEDGEMENT

I would like to express my deepest gratitude to several individuals and resources that made this book possible. First and foremost, I want to acknowledge the crucial role of the large language model that served as my primary writing partner. Its ability to generate creative text, assist with research, and organize complex information was instrumental in shaping this book from concept to reality. This collaboration has truly highlighted the potential of AI as a powerful tool for creators of all kinds.

Beyond the AI assistance, I would also like to acknowledge the contributions of others, both direct and indirect, who have played a part in this project. To any beta readers, friends or colleagues that may have given feedback or input: thank you for your insightful comments and suggestions. This book has greatly benefited from this external perspective.

Finally, I wish to express my appreciation to my family and friends for their patience, encouragement, and understanding throughout the course of this undertaking. It is the support and motivation of loved ones that enable us to take risks and pursue passion projects such as this.

Are you ready to unlock the full potential of Google AI Studio and revolutionize the way you approach AI development? Whether you're a beginner, developer, or tech enthusiast, this comprehensive guide will teach you everything you need to know about Google AI Studio—from the basics to advanced applications.

Packed with detailed explanations, examples, and hands-on exercises, this book is designed to simplify even the most complex AI concepts. Whether you're creating intelligent apps, automating processes, or diving into machine learning, "The Ultimate Guide to Google AI Studio" is your one-stop resource.

This book has been prepared with the information available up to its publication date(November 2025). Please be aware that Google AI Studio is a continuously evolving platform. Therefore, some features, functionalities, and menu names may differ slightly from what is presented herein due to ongoing updates and improvements by Google. We encourage you to explore the latest documentation and interface within Google AI Studio for the most up-to-date information. Discover the Power of Artificial Intelligence with Google AI Studio!

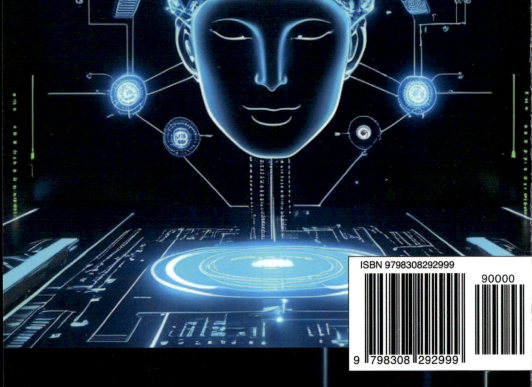

ISBN 9798308292999

90000

9 798308 292999